My Dear Dolphin

BY CYNTHIA DE NARVAEZ

PHOTOGRAPHS BY JERRY GREENBERG

American Heritage Press

NEW YORK

To Robert Corbin, with love,
because he introduced us

INTRODUCTION

THE BOY AND THE DOLPHIN

"Valerius reports that there was a certain boy of fifteen years who daily went to the seashore. Seeing this, a dolphin began to play with the boy and to carry him on his back.

"Daily the boy brought bread to the dolphin and so nurtured the dolphin for four or five years. But it happened one day that the boy went to the seashore carrying bread with him, as he was accustomed. The dolphin did not come and as he waited the sea closed around the boy and he was drowned. When the sea drew back, the dolphin came, and when he found the dead boy, he lay down beside him and died of grief." GESTA ROMANORUM

The potentially close ties between dolphins and people go back, as the quotation from this very old book makes clear, to the days of the ancient Romans. It seems strange, then, that only fitfully in the centuries between then and now have any further attempts been made to explore the remarkable qualities of Brother Dolphin.

The twentieth century has brought a rebirth of interest in this marvelous mammal. Scientific experiments calculated to find out more about his remarkable intelligence and his seemingly instinctive kinship with people are only part of the picture. Another and equally significant aspect of the story is the sheer delight dolphins take in the company of human beings. They invent water games that are as much fun as any land sport you can name. Like the nicest people you know, they are loyal friends, sympathetic companions, on hand to comfort you when you need a helping flipper, sad to see you go away on a long trip. *Unlike* people, they get angry sometimes but they almost never hold a grudge.

Perhaps because, young or old, dolphins have great strength and endurance, they like best to make friends with children who can swim and play in the water all day without getting tired and wanting to flop down at the water's edge to take a nap.

We hope you'll like this true story of four children who spend a school vacation with four dolphins. They had some surprising adventures playing with, and learning about and from, their big friends. Their mother kept this diary of how it all happened.

AMERICAN HERITAGE PRESS

Friday, March 15, was a brilliant day, clear and cool. The sun sparkled off the blue-green water of the pool, flashed from the white-caps in the bay, brightened the colorful clothes of the spectators in the bleachers, and danced on the red and yellow toys that littered the concrete apron at the side of the pool. We sat on the wall in a fever of anticipation. Suddenly a fin knifed up through the water and a gleaming gray body rolled over with a puff and a gasp and was gone.

"There's one! There's one, where did it go?"

A dolphin at last!

The trip from New York that morning had been their first flight for the four children. Ninu, eleven, Cynta, nine, Claudia, six, Felito, four, and I, their mother, were spending our spring vacation near a tourist playground that offered Wild West shows, souvenir shops, and displays of small indigenous birds and animals. What had lured us there, however, was the main attraction, located at the bay end of the area: a pool inhabited by seven large bottle-nosed dolphins. Although we were faithful followers of Flipper, the famous television star, we had never seen live dolphins before.

The dolphin rose again! It gasped. We gasped in unison with it. The animal was much larger than we had imagined, and moved as though it were oiled. We had expected another Flipper, cozy and familiar, but this dolphin was a deep-sea creature, immense, strange, and beautiful.

A young man in white pants and a red and white striped shirt walked out onto the dock. On his shock of sun-bleached hair he wore a cocky little captain's cap. He introduced himself as Michael, the trainer, welcomed us, greeted the dolphin in the pool as Pete, and gave us a brief talk on dolphins. He told us that they are mammals, not fish. They use their mouths mainly for eating; they breathe and speak through the blowhole, or spiracle, at the top of the head, and can drown if water enters the blowhole. Not only is the blowhole the dolphin's "nose," but it contains organs corresponding to our lips, vocal cords, and tongue. The "tongue" serves to close the blowhole when the dolphin dives.

Dolphins die of dehydration if they are out of water for too long.

The permanent "smiling" expression on a dolphin's face seems to show his joyful and friendly disposition.

His intelligence is extremely high. Dolphins almost never fight among themselves, although they are expert shark killers, and they are renowned savers of lives, both dolphin and human.

They are remarkably easy to train, but are apt to become "stage-struck" and turn into prima donnas. They love applause and laughter, and perform best for an appreciative audience.

There are about thirty varieties of dolphins, of which the bottle-nose is one of the largest. They are often called porpoises, which is a mistake, because the porpoise is a smaller species of dolphin that lives only in the Black Sea.

Michael told us that a dolphin's skin is delicate and extremely sensitive. They have keen eyesight in the air and under the sea, and their hearing is such that they can detect sounds ten miles away through the water. Their sense of taste compensates for their lack of sense of smell.

During Michael's introductory speech, Pete, the dolphin in the pool, came close to the dock and lifted his head and body out of the water. He watched Michael with his mouth open in an enormous grin and listened attentively. Michael stressed the fact that dolphins love

Pete

applause and urged everyone to shout and clap loudly if he enjoyed the show. When he finished, Pete squawked and shook his flippers as if to say, "That was great, thank you, but now let's get on with it!"

Telling him to mind his manners, Michael threw him a basketball. Pete fielded it neatly on his beak and sped through the pool toward the basket, which hung nine feet above the water. He tossed the ball and made a perfect goal. We cheered. Michael laughed at someone in the audience who sneered that Pete couldn't do it twice, and returned the ball to the dolphin, who caught it, tossed it, caught it again as it came through the basket, and tossed it a third time. We glowed with pride as if he had been a member of the family.

When Michael told Pete to ring for dinner, he leaped into the air and rang a bell hung high above the water, then raced to the dock to be rewarded with chunks of tender butterfish. Michael then skimmed a mortarboard out on the surface of the pool, and Pete dived under it and came up wearing it on his head at a professorial angle, swam to the dock, and delivered it to Michael.

To demonstrate a dolphin's extraordinary sonar system, the trainer showed us a quarter, then tossed it far out into the water. Pete dived on

Basket!

command, making rapid clicking noises through his blowhole, and soon returned with the quarter in his beak. Then, to prove that the pool was not lined with quarters, Michael dropped his waterproof watch into the pool. Without a moment's hesitation Pete retrieved it.

Slipping into a grass skirt thrown to him by the trainer, the eager dolphin danced a wild hula on his tail. Then he assumed a menacing air, with a huge cowboy hat over his eyes and a gun in a holster cocked over his flippers. He careened down the pool on a round surfboard,

Hula skirt

Cowboy

10

and at the order "Hit the deck," heaved himself full-length out of the water onto a mat on the dock at Michael's feet. There he lay, high and dry, yelling in self-congratulation, and Michael poured the rest of the butterfish into his mouth, then helped him to wriggle back into the pool. Pete knew the whole routine perfectly. He was poised for each trick, radiating excitement, before we had finished applauding the previous one. He moved with fluid ease and joy, and more than earned his fishy rewards, for which he squawked noisily.

While Pete was jumping through the high rings around the edge of the pool, Michael turned to us and said, "You, the lady in the blue dress, will you tell him to jump through the ring?" Pete was right in front of me waiting for his command.

I stammered, "Jump, Pete!" and to my delight he sailed through the ring.

Then Michael asked if any of the children in the audience would care to take a dolphin-powered boat ride. Many children raised their

High and dry

11

hands, including all of mine, and he beckoned to my eldest daughter, Ninu, and to one other child. As the two ran around to the dock, an unoccupied rowboat detached itself from its moorings and moved rapidly across the pool. Pete sat up on his tail with the painter in his mouth and extended it to Michael. The trainer pulled the boat up on the dock, but before the children climbed aboard he introduced them to Pete, who rolled on his side and offered a flipper to be shaken. When they were seated in the boat, Michael eased it into the water and Pete took the painter once more, then tore around the thirty-yard-long pool, pulling the boat behind him. The children sat frozen with delight and terror. Pete returned the boat to the dock, the children climbed out, and the dolphin waved good-by to them with his flipper as they thanked him. Ninu rejoined us, glowing, and Pete retired into his pen at the side of the pool.

For the high-jumping acts that followed, Michael released from their pens two enormous dolphins, Simo and Beau Brummel. Carrying a pail of fish, the trainer climbed the ladder on the concrete apron. When he reached the small platform at the top he propped himself against the railing and leaned way out over the pool. He told the dolphins to get ready. They had been lazing about, watching his preparations, but when he called to them they began to scallop through the water together, in perfect rhythm, faster and faster. Michael cried, "Let's GOOOO!" and they dived. There was a moment of silence and then they exploded out of the water to fly eighteen feet straight up and reach the fish in Michael's hands. They came down with a tremendous splash and the audience burst into roars of delight. They

Simo and Beau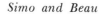

12

jumped several times more and then Michael put Simo back into his pen and raised the ladder six feet higher. We waited breathlessly and saw Beau Brummel shoot out of the water like a guided missile to remove a fish from Michael's mouth.

When the show was over we went around to the dock to thank Michael. My dark-haired, green-eyed Ninu was flushed and boisterous with excitement. She burst out breathlessly, "Michael, please, may we swim with them? Please, when no one else is around, please, may we?"

Michael looked at each of us carefully and said hesitantly, "It's

against all the rules, but . . . possibly," and again, with surprise at himself in his voice, but more positively, "Possibly!"

He led us to a nearby pen to meet Dove, a female dolphin who does no tricks but is everyone's pet. We lay on our stomachs at the side of her pool and dipped our hands in the water. Coasting on her side, she slid slowly toward us. As she approached, Ninu and Cynta retreated, but Claudia reached out to her and trailed her fingers along her head. Dove nudged our hands with her beak, then rubbed against them to coax us to stroke her. She rolled luxuriously over onto her back to be rubbed on the neck and scratched gently between her flippers. Felito patted her, and finally the two older girls, although they were more aware of the dolphin's sharp teeth, dared to join in the massage. Dove grinned at us and turned over a little further to make sure we didn't miss a single inch of her cool skin, softer than that of a baby. Her flippers and dorsal fin felt like smooth, hard rubber. Her back was a dark, silvery gray, blending into the purest blue-white and then to pink-white on her belly. Her face and throat were marked with graceful designs. Michael stood behind us and watched intently.

How reluctant we were to leave when the last tourist train chugged up and hooted at us, "Hurry! It's time to go!" And how glad when Michael invited us to return early in the morning before show time! We assured him we would arrive with the sun, and he told us of a road that led directly to the pool.

Sunday

On Saturday it rained, but at eight o'clock Sunday morning we were once again sitting on the wall, and this time Michael sat with us, as Tom, his assistant, was in charge of the show. He talked with each of us in turn for some time and seemed to be sizing us up and judging our reactions to his beloved animals. When Tom asked which children wished to ride in the boat, Michael signaled to him that Felito was to ride. My four-year-old boarded the boat pale and wide-eyed and clutched the seat with both hands, but presently he relaxed and enjoyed his trip.

We must all have passed Michael's inspection, because at the end of the show he invited us to swim with Pete. We all accepted at once, and Ninu ran around to the dock, tearing off the shirt she was wearing over her bathing suit. But when she faced the huge animal lying in the water she stopped. She turned big eyes on me and shrank a few steps back.

"Swim to the end of the pool and wait," ordered Michael, unaware of her fear.

"Oh, Mummy!" she whispered.

"Go on, Ninu," I quavered. "If you don't, I will!"

That was a real challenge and she plunged into the water, swam across the pool, and waited, treading water. Pete stayed near the dock and watched her, apprehensive about the intruder in his pool.

Michael said quietly, "Go get her, Pete," and Pete disappeared soundlessly underwater.

"Where is he?" Ninu called, searching the pool around her. Pete's big fin rose right in front of her face. She yelped.

Ninu and Pete

"Take hold of his fin and hang on tight," Michael called, laughing.

She did, and Pete, lunging through the water, pulled her straight to the dock.

Ninu climbed out gasping and happy, and Claudia pushed in a horrified Cynta. She thrashed across the pool as though there were devils after her and found Pete waiting at the other side. He dived and slowly spiraled up her body while she squealed and squirmed, then he presented his fin and returned her to the dock. He let her hug him and twittered at her, nodding his head.

Then he shot out of the way as I fell into the chilly pool. Felito had pushed me! I swam to the appointed spot to find that Pete had preceded me and was waiting to tow me back. Traveling on a torpedo might give the same sensation of effortless power.

Cynta squeaked and squirmed.

16

Pete offers Cynta his fin.

Pete waiting for the author

Next we visited with Dove. As I entered the water in her pen she slid under my arm to be hugged, burbling with pleasure at having company. She twisted and snaked around each one of us and then floated on her back, flipping gently around and smiling contentedly. Each time one of us swam toward the side of her pen to get out, she eased herself between the edge and the swimmer, complaining bitterly at being deserted. We had no fear of getting tired in the water because we used her to rest on as she towed us around. Once Ninu wrapped her arms and legs tightly around her, and she began to roll like a hot dog on a spit, with Ninu spinning around and around with her, holding her breath when she was below and spluttering and laughing when she was on top. At last I eased Dove out into the middle of her pool so that the children could get out. She offered no resistance as I rolled her over and rubbed her stomach. Then I sank her gently and climbed out right over her. She drifted on her side, keening with dis-

appointment, and we assured her that we would see her the next day.

The weather was so bad during the first week of our stay that we all had to wear wet suits in order to stay in the water for any length of time. Dove was used to these black rubberlike "union suits" because Michael wore one to dive to the bottom of her pen to clean the filters on the pump that delivered a constant supply of fresh water to the big pool.

The other dolphins, however, must have thought that the wet suits were menacing, and they stayed far away from us at first when we wore them. The black fabric of a wet suit appears very similar to sharkskin, although it is soft and supple. Simo was the first one brave enough to test the suits, and when he found that they were harmless he became as playful as before. Even he, however, much preferred us without them, and when the sun appeared toward the end of our stay, we shed them, and everyone was relieved.

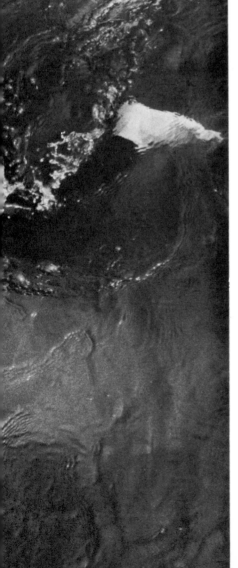

Claudia and Dove

Michael drove us home in his pickup truck. The four children climbed into the back with his three large dogs, and I rode in the cab with him. On the way he told me how he had started training dolphins. Several years ago a friend of his had caught a female dolphin that he thought was more talented than most. He wanted to find out how much she could learn and he invited Michael to come and help him train her.

The dolphin, Mitzi, astonished the men with her abilities. She needed no training; she invented trick after trick, and used every toy they gave her in countless ways. When they liked something she did they rewarded her and added the new trick to her steadily growing repertory. Finally she was "discovered" and became Flipper, the dolphin television star. Michael fell in love with dolphins because of her. He became trainer in a carnival where the public was allowed to swim with the dolphins (those who dared), and when this Florida playground had been established, he had been hired as chief trainer there.

Michael told me about Dr. John C. Lilly and his research into communication with dolphins. Dr. Lilly feels that dolphins are as intelligent as men and possibly more so. He is well on his way to proving his theories with intensive scientific experiments. He has shown that a dolphin's brain is forty per cent larger than the human brain and has more convolutions. Although the thought patterns of dolphins are totally different, their reactions to stimuli are many times faster than ours.

One of the most interesting areas of study is the enormously developed auditory lobes in a dolphin's brain. They use hearing to "see" what is around them in the water. In the murkiest surroundings they are aware of a threatening shark—his distance, size, and how hungry he is—long before they can actually see him. A mother dolphin can use her sonar system to detect uncomfortable air pockets in her baby's stomach and so knows exactly where to give him a gentle poke with her beak to "bubble" him. Blindfolded, a dolphin can easily jump through hoops in the air or find a fish in the water. The United States Navy is devoting serious research to the dolphin's sonar system because it is much more efficient than anything that man has been able to develop.

As we drove along, Michael told me many stories of dolphins' behavior with each other and with people. He told me one about a captive dolphin that was being put into a tank by two handlers when he struggled suddenly, hit his head on the side of the tank, and landed in the water unconscious. He sank and would have drowned had not two dolphins already in the pool rushed down to the bottom to rescue him. Flanking him, they shouldered him to the surface so that he could breathe. He was too heavy for them to support him for very long and they had to let him sink again. They followed him and began to tickle his sides and belly with their flippers. This caused his flippers and tail to move in reflex action, like a dog whose hind legs jerk when you scratch his sides. This motion brought him back to the surface where they continued tickling him until he regained consciousness and was able to move by himself. Then all three leaped and danced to celebrate their joy at his recovery.

Michael told me how wild dolphins all over the world have helped to herd fish into fishermen's nets, and have come in from the sea to play with children in shallow water. He told me about Pelorus Jack, the famous dolphin who guided the ships through Cook Strait in New Zealand for more than twenty years. He was so valuable as a pilot that a law was passed protecting him and all other dolphins in that part of the world.

Monday

When we arrived at the pool this morning we found that Pete had been joined by Simo and Beau Brummel, the two high jumpers. When they saw us they grouped around the dock, staring, creaking, squawking, and smiling. They were very curious about us, but distant, until

Michael gave Felito their hard rubber ball. Seeing this, they yelled with excitement and danced backward on their tails, teasing him to throw it to them. Felito threw the ball and they crashed after it. The pool exploded with spray when they reached it, but there was no argument. The one who got there first got the ball, and in spite of their riotous behavior, we noticed that neither of the others tried to snatch it away from him. They all swooped back and the winner tossed the ball to Felito to have it thrown again. The little boy fumbled and dropped the ball, at which all four children tumbled onto each other on the dock, scrambling and fighting for possession. The victor leaped to her feet and threw the ball as hard as she could, with the others climbing all over her, reaching and wailing. They played the game for an hour or more, the dolphins amicably sharing the ball and watching with fascination as the children fought over it. I was slightly embarrassed. Who was *really* civilized?

Finally the dolphins tired of the game. They slid to the dock on their sides and inspected us with one eye, squeaking to each other and showing us all their teeth. Occasionally one would sit up in the water and nod and talk to us. None of the dolphins would let us touch them, although they came very close. If we reached toward them, they would rapidly snap air, and as they have eighty-eight very sharp teeth, this gave us pause. When we put out our hands to touch a dorsal fin, they sank little by little, always staying a fraction of an inch away. Soon

Beau Brummel   *Simo*

Duncan   Pete   Beau   Simo

Beau Brummel

23

Ninu, Cynta, and I joined them in the water, which alarmed them. They tore around the pool at high speed, but soon decided that we did not seem too dangerous and came closer, circling each one of us. At long last they let us touch them.

Pete preferred Cynta from the first. Pete's beak was short and very scarred. He was tough and battered, almost ugly, if any dolphin can be called ugly. He was a natural impresario as well as the star of the show. My blonde Cynta is small-boned with delicate features and dark, tilted eyes. She too is an impresario. The dolphin and the little girl seemed to be kindred spirits. Perhaps the ham actor in each called out to the other. Pete was not interested in the rest of us, and Cynta was not in the least aware of the other dolphins.

Beau Brummel made friendly advances to Ninu. He lunged up under her so that she found herself riding him, looking like the statue "The Boy on the Dolphin." Then he turned mischievous, shook himself like a wet dog, and dumped her off, but always near the dock. The dolphins seemed to prefer the children to me, but Michael told me this was always the case at first, and not to worry, that one of them would soon adopt me. He made it clear that I had no choice which one it would be. The choice is always theirs. I felt like a puppy in a litter up for sale.

They delighted in playing tricks on us and left us choking with laughter. They disappeared at one end of the pool while we searched for them at the other. Then one of the children flew into the air screaming as a dolphin shot up under her, throwing her as high in the air as he could. Another sped up behind Ninu and dived over her head, coming down flat on his side in front of her and sending an

Pete and Cynta

Pete

enormous wave over all of us. They teased with proffered fins, then streaked away before one of us could grab them. They tossed the ball toward us to see the children scramble, then scooped it away at lightning speed before any of them could touch it. They kept up a constant excited conversation. Mischievous as they were and very rough among themselves, they were never too rough with us. As I was watching them play with the children and thinking about getting out because the water was so cold, I felt a blow on the top of my head, then the ball landed in front of my face in the water, and a great weight settled on my shoulder. Simo had bounced the ball on my head, and with his head and neck resting on my shoulder, was peering around into my face to see my reaction. I burst out laughing and hugged him, at which he produced a sound so exactly like my laugh that I was startled. I hoped this one would adopt me!

Claudia and Felito, who were too small to swim alone in the fifteen-foot-deep pool, cried that they wanted to swim with the dolphins too,

Simo laughed too.

so I took them in, one at a time, with Dove. She was very quiet and gentle with them and solid as a rock, but they gasped at the cold water and at her enormous size. She moved close to them, making comforting noises, and they held on to her. Soon they relaxed and began to pat her, and she swam slowly around her pen, letting them ride her. While Claudia was in the pool, Dove turned over on her back, her favorite position, and I laid my six-year-old on her belly. Dove immediately stuck both flippers straight up in the air to prevent her falling off and sailed like a frigate in a calm sea with Claudia cuddled blissfully

Claudia and Dove

27

against her. The little girl stayed in the pen with Dove longer than her brother did.

To Felito all animals were new and interesting. There were so many things for him to see and do around the pool that he was perfectly content not to swim in deep water. He played with Michael's dogs, built Indian villages with the conical paper cups from the dispenser, and with Claudia, found a pair of wild kittens, which they tamed until they lay inside the children's shirts, purring like lawn mowers.

Felito's happiest moment came when he discovered the two sea lions, Walter and Henery, who lived in a pen not far from the pool. Most people overlooked them because of the charm of the dolphins, but he fed them, and talked to them by the hour, and gave them more love than they had ever enjoyed before. Thereafter, when they saw him coming, they would shuffle as fast as they could to the side of their pen and bark with joy.

Michael's dogs haunted the pool and loved to dive in to chase the dolphins, who swam around them and teased them mercilessly. They danced on their tails within inches of the dogs' noses. They let them get close enough to lunge, then dived between their front legs, past their snapping jaws, and splashed water in their faces. The dogs charged them again and again until, wild with frustration, the three would have to be pulled out before they drowned from exhaustion.

Walter and Henery

28

Cynta and Pete monopolized the ball this morning, so Simo and Beau Brummel came to the dock to visit me. They bobbed up and down in the water, looking like a pair of synchronized yo-yos. I wondered if I could make them jump. I mimicked their motion with my hands: up-down, up-down, up-down, and then swung my arms high over my head. They flew into the air! As the children laughed and applauded, they jumped higher and higher, then, naughty as always, slammed down sideways on the surface of the water and drenched us.

The game ended when we were so wet that we joined them in the

Yo-yos

Persuasion

water. Ninu wanted to swim underwater and dived down headfirst. Beau shot after her and thrust her firmly to the surface.

"It looks as though he doesn't want you to do that, Ninu," I called to her. "But try again to make sure." She dived and popped up again immediately. Beau rested just under her forbiddingly. It was the first time the dolphins had exercised their authority in the water. They made it very clear that none of us was allowed below the surface. Perhaps they thought we would drown.

We were beginning to be able to tell the dolphins apart. We recognized Pete from the beginning. Beau Brummel, well over eight feet long and weighing more than four hundred and fifty pounds, was the most beautiful of them all. He was totally unmarked and unscarred, in spite of having skin so delicate that the slightest scratch could leave a permanent scar. He had a streamlined grace and smoothness that the others could not match. Beau was the "unrequited lover" of the group. He longed to claim Ninu, but she was feeling the first twinges of

Beau

adolescence and preferred to follow Michael around while he did his chores. She was not in the pool enough to let herself be adopted. Then poor Beau decided Claudia might be his cup of tea. He tried to pull her into the pool one morning as she was sitting on the dock dreaming and dangling her feet in the water. He slid silently toward her underwater and eyed her hopefully, then opened his mouth and closed it gently around her ankles. She looked down at him in amazement and squeaked as she began to slide off the dock. He released her at once and squawked at her mournfully. She threw herself flat on the dock, and gathering his big head in her arms, she hugged him, crooning. But she was too small to swim in the deep water, so Beau Brummel pined.

Claudia and Beau (Simo watching)

31

Simo was second only to Beau in beauty and size. He had one or two scars, but it was the gouge in his chin that distinguished him. Simo was a true gentleman. He played tricks for my amusement as well as his own and watched my every reaction intently. He liked to tease by pretending to snap because he knew I was afraid of his teeth. I envied Michael's casual handling of the dolphins and was angry at myself for my fear. Michael assured us that unless brutally ill-treated, no dolphin will injure a human being in any way. Simo never left my side when I was in the water and he kept a fond eye on me wherever else in the vicinity of the pool I happened to be.

We were all having such a lovely time that we hated to leave today.

Tuesday

This morning I scratched Simo casually under one flipper and he shuddered violently, shook, dived, leaped into the air, and tore around in circles. He was ticklish! Ninu was delighted and threw herself into the pool, wrapped her arms around Beau Brummel, and began to tickle him. He bucked like a wild horse and gave her the roughest

Simo was ticklish.

ride of her life. She ended up drowning with laughter as he escaped to the other end of the pool and turned somersaults to recover.

Cynta was playing tag with Pete when he began swimming in tight circles around her, faster and faster. Cynta was sure that it was still a game and tried in vain to catch hold of his fin. Then her laugh turned into a grimace of fright. Pete sensed her sudden fear and slowed down instantly. He coasted, still in tight circles, to a stop. He looked in her face and patted her gently with his flippers until she smiled at

Pete swam around her in tight circles.

He slowed down.

him with relief, then he offered her his fin and slalomed easily around
the pool with the little girl in tow. We never knew what he might
have had in mind, but it obviously didn't work and he never tried it
again.

In the meantime, Felito and Claudia had boarded the rowboat,
which was moored at one end of the pool. Unseen and unsuspected,
Beau Brummel pulled the slipknot of the painter, and before they
knew what was happening they were out in the middle of the pool.
Everyone was delighted except for the kitten nestled in Claudia's lap.
He mewed in panic and scrambled under her shirt, where he could
make believe he was on dry land. Beau pulled them all around the

In the middle of the pool

pool and then dropped the painter near Simo, who towed them around again. Pete continued the trip when the rope was dropped near him.

Wednesday

Today when we arrived, the dolphins chatted as if we had not seen them in a month and they had to tell us everything at once. Ordinarily they don't interrupt each other, but this morning they were all talking at once. They were so active that they looked like fourteen dolphins in the pool, so at first we didn't realize that there were actually four instead of three!

Duncan, a dolphin that made us all a little nervous, had escaped from his pen in the night. We had been careful with him because he allowed no one to approach him, not even Michael, and he often tried to knock us into the water when we slipped past his pen on the catwalk. On one occasion Simo had entered Duncan's pen and they had had a terrible battle. (This is unusual among dolphins because it is almost impossible to make them fight.) Michael had had to jump on them to separate them.

When something makes a dolphin angry he punishes with a nip or a slap of the tail and then forgets the incident entirely. Duncan was covered with battle scars, many from that fight with Simo, but most dating from before his capture. We learned that he had been a member of a high-jump act with Simo and Beau Brummel. One day he refused to jump. He did not interfere with the big dolphin, Beau, but he took to breaking Simo's jumps by interrupting the latter's underwater preparations. Finally he was taken out of the act and had not worked since, but Simo had never forgiven him.

Now here was Duncan in the pool and we were apprehensive. He

Duncan

had watched us playing and couldn't bear to be left out any longer. Even Michael seemed uneasy. He knew that only a net could force Duncan back into his pen, but a net would terrify all the dolphins and ruin the day, both for us and for the performances. The trainer stayed close by the pool all morning, instead of working in the fish house as usual.

I greeted Simo, and Duncan approached to look at me with intense curiosity and a tentative friendliness. The children drew back from the water's edge and Simo shouldered Duncan away from me. He stayed persistently between Duncan and me and even threatened to bite him. Poor Duncan! He looked lonely and seemed eager to make friends. He watched us playing with his mates but never tried to join in. Finally (and foolishly) I scolded Simo and waved him out of the way. He drifted off and watched from a distance as Duncan swam up to me, chirping, and let me pet him. Duncan had a very protuberant lower jaw, giving him a rather bull-doggish aspect, and black teeth, which Michael said was a sign of old age. He certainly didn't behave in an elderly way. Soon I called Simo. He came slowly, reluctant to

Simo shouldered Duncan away.

37

resume an interrupted friendship immediately. For the rest of the day he ignored Duncan. That night, however, he entered Duncan's pen and tried to kill him. If Michael's assistant had not heard the commotion in his cabin by the pool and rushed out to separate them, something tragic would have happened. If only I had realized that it was wise to follow Simo's wishes rather than my own!

This was not the only mistake I made today! Simo and I were playing ball. Usually when he threw the ball to me I missed it and would have to scramble all over the dock to retrieve it and throw it back to him. I never took it out of his mouth, not because I knew better, but because he never gave me the opportunity. This time, however, he lifted his head to me with the ball in his beak. I grabbed it and pulled, and he whipped his head away from me, retaining the ball. He moved out of reach and started bouncing the ball up and down in his mouth, keeping one eye on me. I thought he was teasing, and when he bounced it a little higher I reached out and snatched it, laughing, and fell into the pool. He whirled in the water, obviously angry, and brought his tail down in a tremendous slap right next to me. Then he moved away and would have nothing more to do with me. It was only after the return of the ball and an hour of cajoling that he became friendly

I reached out and snatched the ball.

again. After that he behaved as though he had forgotten the whole incident. He seemed to take the attitude that though hopelessly ignorant, I was still lovable. Even when dolphins are being fed they never snatch the fish out of the trainer's hand. They wait until he drops it into their mouths, or hold it very lightly until he lets go. Simo expected the same courtesy from me.

Thursday

The first thing we noticed on our arrival this morning was poor Duncan's condition. He was slashed and cut and bleeding in several places, but his spirits seemed high. Although we were all horrified when we heard about the fight, it cleared the air between the two dolphins, and they appeared to be on friendly terms at last. Simo was in a beautiful mood! He was relaxed, joyful, and playful to such an extent that when, as I frolicked with him in the pool, he took my hand in his beak and mouthed it gently, my feeling was one of great relief. He must have felt the same, because he then rubbed his head against mine and patted me with his flippers to show his joy that I was no longer afraid. He never snapped at me again.

Surfing

Dolphins love to surf! Pete used the round board as a regular act in the show, but the others had not tried it before and became tremendously excited when they saw us carry it to the end of the dock. We heaved it across the pool and Beau Brummel lunged onto it, thrashing his tail furiously. He surfed all the way down the pool with spray flying in all directions. He fell off, and Simo, who had sped after him underwater, threw himself onto the board and with equal agility rode it in the opposite direction. On the dock we were jumping up and down, screaming with delight and wishing we could do it too, when Michael came out of the fish house to see what all the commotion was about. Even he was flabbergasted at their shenanigans.

Ninu climbed to the top of the ladder, high over the pool, and holding out her sandals, called to Simo and Beau to jump for them. The enormous dolphins scalloped faster and faster together around the pool, dived to the bottom, and exploded into the air, twenty feet high,

Ninu's view from the ladder

to touch lightly the sandals with their beaks and crash down into the
water again. From her vantage point it was breath-taking! Duncan
watched. He would not jump, but he didn't interfere with Simo.

What amazed us was that while the show was on they yelled like
children for their fish after each trick, but they never once demanded

Reading up: Felito, Claudia, Cynta, Ninu; then down: Beau and Simo

a reward from us! As a matter of fact, Michael never allowed us to feed them for fear of slowing down their performances at show time, but our delight and praise were apparently reward enough.

When we try to teach them something new they need only a hint to guess the trick we have in mind. The children take their intelligence

*Brill,
above,
and
Tessa, right,
and Brill again,*

for granted, but I find myself feeling very humble as I get to know them better each day.

After the show, Michael invited us to go out to sea on the *Harbor Queen,* an old stern-wheel riverboat, to watch the two dolphins from the sea pens at work. These were two lovely small females, still in the process of being trained, whose names were Tessa and Brill. Michael told us that they specialized in dancing and jumping at high speeds, and that their act was what wild dolphins often do around ships at sea. We boarded the boat along with all the spectators, and stayed on the lower of the two decks in order to get a better view of the proceedings. Michael released the dolphins and they bounded out into the bay as he started the boat. After a moment's taste of freedom, they swung back to the boat and circled it happily as it moved out to sea. They plunged into the wave raised by the bow as it cut through the water, and relaxing on their sides, hitched a free ride and grinned up at us. Suddenly Tessa, the smaller dolphin, plunged directly in front of the boat and we gasped with fear that she would be run over. But she matched the speed of the boat and then flung herself into the air and danced on a wildly flipping tail, sending floods of water over all of us on the lower deck. Brill joined her to drench us further, but we didn't mind a bit. We were busy trying to figure out how they could remain upright, dancing, and still maintain their

circle
the Harbor Queen

speed! Too soon the boat came about and started back. At that the dolphins separated and swam on either side of the vessel. Michael and his assistant hung over the railings on opposite sides of the high second deck and held out butterfish to the dolphins. Tessa and Brill leaped, one after the other, all the way up to take the fish. They jumped repeatedly and never lost their swimming stride or dropped behind the boat. When we reached the pier they went straight into their pens and yelped for applause and reward.

This evening Michael told us that the board of directors was coming down over the weekend and we couldn't visit the dolphins.

Saturday

We spent the day at the beach and explored the surrounding countryside for the first time since we have been here. Tonight at dinner in the hotel, Michael came to our table looking harassed. "Oh, man, what a day I've had!" He shook his head. "They wouldn't perform! They looked for you and called for you all morning, and when show time came along, they wouldn't do a thing!" He groaned. "Beau missed his high jump *three times* and then refused to try again. Pete forgot half his routine and went under the dock and sulked. Simo was unruly and rebellious. They wouldn't do anything they were supposed to do, and all the directors were there! After all they have heard about my dolphins this had to happen! And they kept it up during *all three shows.*" Poor Michael. He still has to get through Sunday. So do we.

Sunday

Today we collected sunburns and a million sea shells, all of which Claudia expects to take back to New York. This evening Michael came by again, looking only slightly less distraught than yesterday. The shows had not been as bad, but the dolphins were listless and slow. Again they had spent the morning searching and calling for us. What will happen when we leave?

I came down with the flu tonight: no voice and a high fever. Somehow we managed. Ninu and Cynta bathed and dressed the two little ones and took them down to the hotel dining room, where all of them, I was told later, displayed the most exemplary table manners and were far, far more civilized than they ever are when I'm with them. All four were as good to me and to each other as if they had been dolphins. What good influences one's friends can be! The doctor ordered me to stay in bed for at least three days.

Monday

Feeling like a naughty child, I disobeyed the doctor's orders about not getting up. Instead, we all went straight down to the pool this morning. Michael grinned from ear to ear when he saw us, and hugged all the children happily. Claudia found her kittens, which climbed right up her, mewing loudly. Michael gave Felito a pail of cut fish to feed to his sea lions, who were barking frantically. Ninu and Cynta and I rushed down to the dock, only to be met with silence. The dolphins lay under the water in a row and looked at us out of their left eyes. I lay down on the dock fully clothed and Ninu and Cynta eased into the water, afraid that our friends had forgotten us or that they were hurt at our enforced desertion. Then came the explosion! The dolphins burst into the air with yells of joy, then raced under and around and over the children. They behaved as though they couldn't get close enough, and at the same time they couldn't stay still enough to get close.

Simo soon stopped his gleeful dance to join me, curious as to why

*The
explosion*

I didn't come into his pool. He bobbed up and down and I reached my arms around him. He rubbed his cool face against mine. It was difficult to cuddle when one of us was in the water and the other wasn't, but he surely tried. He pushed his head at me repeatedly to persuade me to rub his neck and around his blowhole. As I petted

Simo, my pet

46

him he began to slide very slowly through the water until I was scratching around his fin. One just naturally takes hold of a fin, it's that kind of a handle, and as soon as he felt that I had a firm hold he plunged out into the pool. Had I not been flat on the dock I would have been jerked right into the water. As it was I had to grapple with the dock to stay on it.

I called after him, "What are you doing, you sneaky fish?" and found myself suspended over the water as a furious Michael began to throw me in. He would not stand for his dolphins being called fish.

I coughed at him and squeaked, "Help!" and he relented and put me back on the dock.

Simo watched with interest and then squawked and offered me his fin again. I explained to him why I could not come in, but he tried all kinds of persuasion, including an attempt to drench me with his tail. Finally he gave up. He came very close, and with his beak just inches away from my face, he began to squirt a tiny jet of water at me. It was so surprising and so gentle that I didn't move.

Michael was standing on the dock behind me, and he grinned and said, "You had better do it back. He's kissing you!"

I did, of course, and the children were enchanted as we exchanged wet kisses back and forth. Cynta wanted to try it with Pete, but he was too sophisticated. Every time she tried to spray him he bumped her mouth with his beak, trying to kiss her in the human way. The other dolphins all came to the dock to say hello, and with Simo's kind indulgence, Duncan rubbed faces with me. Michael is constantly amazed at Duncan's gentleness with us.

I got dizzy and then remembered that I was supposed to be in bed. We went home reluctantly.

Tuesday

Michael received a letter this morning from a friend who catches wild dolphins for marine shows. He is a gentle man, wise in the ways of dolphins, and to capture them he either nets them or jumps on them in the water and immobilizes them by grabbing firm hold of the tail—quite a feat! One day he went out hunting dolphins and found a school of mothers with their babies. He hoped that if he caught a young one the mother would follow him home and he would bag two instead of one. He found a lovely newborn baby, just three feet long and identical to its mother, except that it had three or four stiff little whiskers on its tiny beak. He jumped it, caught it, and cradled it in his arms in the water. It didn't seem frightened as he started swimming back to his boat. On the contrary, it was trusting and playful. The mother approached him, whistling, circled him, rubbed against him, and nuzzled the baby. He knew she was trying to persuade him to release it. He spoke to her gently and invited her to come along. She moved away and watched from a little distance, then returned, circled him closely again, pleaded with him more urgently, seeming almost to weep, and pushed at the baby in his arms. Then she sped away and disappeared. He continued toward the boat, wondering at how easy it was, when some instinct made him glance in the direction in which the mother had vanished. She was shooting toward him like a torpedo, on her way to ram and kill him. He released the baby, threw his arms above his head, and said his prayers. The mother stopped short just inches away from him, chirped at the little dolphin, and disappeared with the baby in tow. Shaken and amazed, the man boarded his boat. He knew that any other animal would have killed him without hesitation. Michael was deeply impressed with his friend's account, as was I, but after having known dolphins, even for so short a time, I was not surprised.

Wednesday

Today was busy. Felito supervised the cleaning of the sea lions' pen from a safe distance; sea lions bite. Ninu helped clean out the neighboring pool that Dove was to move into. She slopped water all over Michael until, to the dolphins' delight, he threw her into the big pool. Cynta was in the water playing with Pete, Beau Brummel was pulling Claudia and the seafaring kittens around in the boat, and the dogs were in the sea pens intent on murdering the dolphins there, who were enjoying it immensely.

Still landlocked and fully clothed, I was conversing with Simo from the dock when he swam away toward Pete and whistled at him. Pete dropped the ball in front of him and Simo carried it to the dock, trilled

49

at me, and tossed it. I missed it, and he uttered a sound very like a Bronx cheer, raced around the dock, scooped the ball out of the water, and threw it to me again. He was so fast that I fumbled it again, whereupon he made more rude noises and tried once more. Then I realized that my dolphin was trying to teach his pet (me) to play catch. I missed the ball repeatedly, partly because he moved faster than my eyes could follow him, and partly because I can't play catch. He threw more and more slowly until at last I caught it. At this he reared up, dancing on his tail, shouted congratulations, nodded his head, and clapped his flippers in approval, exactly as he had seen us do at his jumps in the show! I felt as though I had won a prize! He continued

Simo, the teacher

drilling me until I could catch the ball at his speed from any angle. What a teacher! There are not many people who are capable of such quiet perseverance and patience, or who can bring themselves to demonstrate such lavish praise at the final success of their slowest pupil.

Thursday

Today we discovered that Michael is Superman in disguise. He finished scrubbing out Dove's new pool and filled it with water. His assistant brought a big stretcher and laid it on the pavement. Then Michael called Dove to him. She came at once and swooned into his arms as though he were Romeo to her Juliet, and he petted her and murmured sweet nothings. The trainer is tiny. He is one hundred pounds of solid muscle on a five-foot frame. He leaned over her and slowly lifted her three hundred pounds into his arms, then stood up. She lay in his arms like an enormous rag doll, with her eyes shut tight. He carried her to the stretcher and laid her down on it with great care. Then he and his assistant picked up the stretcher and carried her to her new pool, where Michael picked her up again, cuddled her for a moment, and slid her gently into the water. The five of us let out a communal blast of long-held breath.

The pool was a shock to Dove, as it was far too cold for her. She had to keep swimming around and around in order to maintain her body heat. She couldn't even stop to say hello, and as she needed more nourishment in this new environment, Michael let us feed her. She ate on the run, and the trainer told us she would have to keep moving until the pool warmed up, even if it took a day or two.

Friday

Today we had a few misfortunes. Beau had spent some time towing all four children around in the rowboat, and when he tired of it they took turns rowing with an old broken oar that one of them had found in the bottom of the boat. An argument soon arose as to whose turn it was to row and in the midst of it someone swung the oar and clobbered someone else on the side of the head. An instant of stunned silence was followed by howls of pain and rage. I was helpless, as I was still avoiding the water. Michael was cutting up fish in the fish house, too far away to hear, and his assistant had the day off. I yelled to Beau to bring them in, and before the words were out of my mouth he had rushed them to the dock. The victim was not badly hurt and was delighted to have acquired a shiner to take back to school.

The other event was less painful but more frightening. Cynta was playing ball with Pete in the water. She skipped it across the pool for him and as he dived after it Duncan plunged over to her and began to

Drowned

Rescued

Brought in

52

leap around her in circles. As he had never approached any of us in the water before, she was frightened. Duncan had often watched Pete jump over her but had never tried it himself. Now he did, but he jumped so low that his tail knocked her head underwater. She came up screaming. The dolphins collected near me at the dock and twittered and shook their flippers. They were terrified and bewildered. Had she been drowning, all four would have gone to her rescue, but she wasn't drowning, she was just making a fearful noise, and they didn't know what to do. I called to her to try to pull herself together and swim in, but she couldn't seem to hear me. I saw her eyes change then, from desperation to hopelessness, and knowing she was about to sink, I dived off the dock. Before I hit the water, Simo understood and streaked to her side. He brought her back to the dock, plunged underneath her, and shoved her out of the water. Then he came back to me and towed me as well, sodden and shivering, to the dock.

Saturday

Today was our last day with the dolphins.

They were very subdued and stayed as close to us as possible. Michael tried to cheer us up but was so depressed that he could not make a very good job of it. We all tried to memorize every last detail of the pool and its surroundings; above all, of our beloved creatures.

When it was time to go, Cynta stood on the edge of the dock and held her arms out to Pete. He rose out of the water and held himself as still as possible on his tail while she leaned over to take his head in her arms. Tears ran down her face onto his as she kissed him good-by. Each time she started to draw away, Pete pushed himself a little higher to keep her from going. Finally she ran to the car to her misery.

I lay down on the dock and said good-by to all the dolphins and then to my Simo. I hugged and kissed him and finally drew back onto my knees, determined to go. As I knelt, Simo began to bounce, higher and higher, until suddenly he threw himself full-length out of the water onto the dock and lay with his head on my lap. I threw my arms around him and cried. He burbled sadly. At last I helped him back into the water and ran before he could beach himself again. The dolphins were very quiet as we said good-by to Michael and climbed into the car.

One year later we returned to our dolphins. We were anxious to see if they would remember us after all this time. Upon our arrival we hurried to the pool, each of us hunting for her particular friend, and Felito rushed to see his sea lions, Walter and Henery. With some trepidation I approached Simo's pen and knelt down on the concrete at its edge. He rolled over and blew at the far end of his pool, and bobbed up in front of me, staring curiously. Calling his name, I reached my hands out to him. He whistled suddenly and loudly. Coming close, he seized my hand and chewed it gently, tasting who I was. Then, yelping with excitement, he leaped backward with a mighty splash and began to dance wildly around his pen. He turned flip after flip, dived deep down and burst into the air, spun like a top through the water, danced on his tail, and voiced his discovery loudly to his mates. They had just recognized the children and were reacting similarly. The joyous barking of the sea lions mingled with their wild cries as they danced a wild fandango in their pens, yipping like happy puppies, and raced back to their children to be hugged and petted until their excitement overcame them again and they had to explode with glee. As I sat with my feet in the water of his pen, Simo finally calmed and grasped my ankle tenderly. He pushed his big head between my feet and surged and wriggled as I scrubbed his back.

The riverboat, *Harbor Queen*, had been on her way out to sea, loaded with tourists and Michael, when we arrived. Now it returned. Michael jumped onto the dock before the boat was properly berthed, and ran to the pool to greet us with warm hugs and handshakes. Our joy at seeing him was reflected on his tanned and happy face. His hair was much longer and bleached silver, and we all decided that he looked exactly like Robinson Crusoe. He was delighted at the idea and decided then and there to grow a beard.

We stayed for two weeks, and the relationship between the dolphins and us deepened well beyond novelty and fascination. Dove claimed Claudia as though she were her own baby, and became protective toward her to such an extent that the arrival of the tourists brought out a dangerous streak that I would not have thought possible in such a gentle creature. She did not allow Claudia to leave her pool when

The author and Simo

spectators came, but circled her constantly and charged toward the strangers with viciously clacking beak and warning cries. Then she hurried back to Claudia and stayed firmly between her and the intruders. She encouraged the little girl to take her dorsal fin and then quickly towed her as far away from the crowd as was possible. She patted Claudia gently with her flippers, burbling sweet nothings in her ear and rubbing her beak against her face, then turned toward the tourists and yelled imprecations.

We were never supposed to be seen in the water with the dolphins, but as there was no other way to get Claudia out, I eased into Dove's pool to try to retrieve her. Dove lunged between us, trying to force me away from her, chirping at Claudia to stay away from me. The big female knew me and was gentle, but she also knew what I was up to and wanted me nowhere near to "her" baby. At last Claudia climbed

Dove and Claudia

astride her and then fell over into my arms. I carried her out of the pool, leaving Dove wailing and calling to her. I felt like a kidnapper!

Sunday

Beau Brummel did something particularly helpful during his solo high-jump act in the show one day. Michael raised the ladder to its greatest height, maintaining a steady banter with the audience as was his habit, but he forgot to joggle the supporting bar of the ladder into position. This meant that the ladder could drop six inches while he was atop the platform, throwing him into the water twenty-four feet below and possibly injuring him. As he started to climb, Beau yelled loudly at him and clapped his flippers together.

"What ails you?" Michael shouted. "Get into position, knuckle-head!"

Beau yelled again and turned two flips under the ladder. Michael came down the step or two that he had already taken. He looked at the ladder and quickly realized what the problem was.

"Why, thanks, old man," he called to the worried dolphin. "You just saved me a bump on the head!"

Beau fell on his back and clapped his flippers together happily as Michael adjusted the ladder into a safe position. The audience gasped in appreciation and wonder.

Tuesday

One cold and cloud-covered day, Claudia climbed into her little black wet suit and prepared to swim with Dove. (At this time Dove was occupying the harbor pens, all alone. Tessa and Brill had been sold during the summer, and Michael had to have someone to work with the riverboat, so Dove had been chosen. Dove was accustomed to crowds of people lavishing her with attention and love, and in the harbor pens she was all alone and she felt it. Claudia swam with her there every day for hours to keep her happy.) The little girl got ready and hurried over to Dove's pen and called to her. Nothing happened. She was about to call to her again when she noticed that part of the fence enclosing the pen from the harbor had fallen down. She screamed. Dove was gone! We all left what we were doing and rushed to Claudia, trying to find out what was the matter. She burst into tears and pointed at the broken fence.

Michael went white. He ran to the phone in the cabin on the dock and called the captain of the riverboat, who said that he would come immediately to help hunt for her. We all got on the boat and waited in silence. Finally the captain appeared. We covered Dove's usual working area but she was nowhere to be found. We saw three splashes a distance away and hurried to investigate them. One was a pelican fishing. The others were two wild dolphins playing with an empty beer can.

A heavy rain began to fall. Michael paced up and down in the cabin, anxious and fearful. When he sat down and put his head in his hands, Felito went to him and put his arms around his shoulders. This almost unmanned him, but he hugged the little boy and then lunged out to pace the deck in the rain.

When he came back in he told us that Dove had been caught when she was just barely weaned, at two years old, and that she had never learned how to catch her own fish. If she didn't come back she would starve to death. The captain rumbled that she would surely come back when she got hungry, but we knew that if she had met a herd of wild dolphins she would go with them, Heaven knew how far. The captain came about well past the end of Dove's usual working run, and we returned to the dock filled with gloom.

When we arrived we found the manager of the tourist center waiting for us impatiently. He had just received a phone call.

"She's up at Ken's Fish Club on Midnight Pass Road," he called. "You'll have to get a small boat to get in there!"

Michael didn't stop to argue. He was sure he would find a boat at the Fish Club. We leaped into the car and sped out of the grounds onto the freeway. The ten-mile ride took five minutes in spite of the rain. We found the Fish Club, parked, and ran around to the dock. There we found twenty or more delighted people. Dove was in the water in front of the dock, happy as a bird, mugging and showing off, reveling in the kind of attention she had missed for so long. She loved to swim with fast-moving boats and she had found one and followed it to this most hospitable place. People had been feeding her shrimp (her favorite delicacy) and chunks of fresh fish, and she had entertained them lavishly for their kindness.

58

We rushed to the end of the dock and Dove promptly stopped clowning and looked at us with one abashed and guilty eye. She saw Claudia and sat up and squeaked happily, inviting her to join in the fun. Claudia burst into wails of relief at seeing her, and Michael looked as though he wanted to do the same. We all felt the same way.

Most of the people on the dock knew who Michael was, but we heard some whispers behind us: "Who are they? Who are those children? What do they have to do with this?"

"These are the Dolphin Children!" Michael announced loudly, and he herded them onto the boat that had led Dove in and followed them aboard. The boat's owner had very kindly offered to take Dove back to her pen. The boat started away with Dove bouncing alongside, then she turned and circled back to the dock. She did a lovely flip to thank her admirers, then cocked a mischievous eye at me, squawked and nodded her head as if to say, "See you later," and tore away in pusuit of the boat.

I drove back to the pool at a leisurely pace and waited for the triumphal procession to arrive. The captain and I waited out of the rain in the cabin of the riverboat. Finally we heard a distant "Halloo!" and in they came, Dove leaping ahead of the boat, proud of and pleased with her adventure. Michael fixed the pen and then there were joyous hugs all around. Dove was home safe!

*Michael
and
no
Dove*

Claudia and Dove returned

The dolphins became quite rambunctious at times. They loved to play leapfrog and we were the frogs! One and then two at a time went hurtling over our heads as we howled with terror and glee! Two would jump in opposite directions, and then one, two, three, in rapid succession!

They played a game we called Whirlpool, with two or three of them spinning around one of us as fast as they could go until they created a whirlpool with the victim at the bottom of it, spinning in spite of herself. When they had it going as fast as they wanted it, they could move us anywhere they wanted, helplessly caught! This must have been what Pete was working up to with Cynta last year. We knew them so much better now that none of us was frightened. It was fun having them boss us around and they certainly thought so too!

On occasion Simo would start shoving and bumping me, flipping

Leapfrog

60

over backward if I tried to take his fin, bumptious and stubborn, until I went limp in the water and said to him, "All right, I'm just going to lie here in the water and not do anything at all." That was exactly what he wanted. He tickled me and pushed me around a bit to see if I really meant it, and when I didn't move he took my arm in his mouth and towed me around the pool. He ferried me to each of the jumping rings and to each of the pens, then deposited me in the exact center of the pool and jumped over my stomach a few times. I still didn't move and he was delighted. He tried pushing me sideways, holding me by the leg, but that was too slow, so he took my arm again and dropped me off at the dock. After all this he was content to let me hug him and pet him. He had proven some point to himself. Maybe he was a little unsure as to who was whose pet. There was no doubt now!

Simo and the author

61

Our experience with the dolphins was the same as last year's and yet different. The same because all the animals involved were the same, but different because of the deep trust and familiarity that grow between old friends revisited. Michael allowed Ninu to make Dove jump for fish on the riverboat. Claudia and Felito had exclusive feeding

Ninu and Dove

rights to the sea lions and Dove, and they gave some of Dove's dinner to three pelicans and a cormorant who ate out of their hands.

The two little ones were big enough and had learned to swim well enough to join the dolphins in the big pool. Claudia loved their games and was never afraid, and so did Felito, but he preferred me to hold him or to stay close. Cynta found that the other dolphins were almost as charming as her Pete, and, although she will always prefer him, she enjoyed playing with the others as well.

It was clear the last day that they knew we were leaving. They must have sensed our sadness, as they were particularly gentle and loving and particularly funny. They all claimed all of us, and we took turns being towed at remarkable speed by two dolphins at the same time! How lovely it is to swim around a pool with two fins cutting the water on either side offering company and protection. Our leave-taking was sad, but it wasn't the terrible, wrenching departure of last year, when none of us knew whether we would ever see each other again. We

Felito preferred to stay close to me.

all know now that we will be back again and again. When we left them they were clowning with a ball and a baseball hat, trying to make us laugh.